Reasons to Leave the Slaughter
a collection of poetry

☙

by Ben Clark

Write Bloody Publishing
America's Independent Press

Long Beach, CA

writebloody.com

Copyright © Ben Clark 2011

No part of this book may be used or performed without written consent from the author, if living, except for critical articles or reviews.

Clark, Ben.
1st edition.
ISBN: 978-1-935904-32-8

Interior Layout by Lea C. Deschenes
Cover Designed by Debra Kayes
Cover Photo by Todd Brown
Interior Illustrations by Joshua Cotter
Proofread by Patty Petelin
Edited by Elise Paschen, Sherry Antonini and Marty McConnell
Type set in Helvetica by Linotype, Aller and Bergamo: www.theleagueofmoveabletype.com

Special thanks to Lightning Bolt Donor, Weston Renoud

Printed in Tennessee, USA

Write Bloody Publishing
Long Beach, CA
Support Independent Presses
writebloody.com

To contact the author, send an email to writebloody@gmail.com

For Kate

REASONS TO LEAVE THE SLAUGHTER

REASONS TO LEAVE THE SLAUGHTER

Pasture 15

Apology 16

Fishing 17

At One Hundred, A Miracle 18

Night Shift 20

There's A Beast Roaming 21

The Architecture Of Obsession 21

Breaking 25

Mother 27

What We Do For Fun Around Here #1 28

Death/Wish 29

Summer 32

On Your Birthday 33

What We Do For Fun Around Here #2 35

Father 36

My Father Explains His Birth 37

To My First Love's Soon-To-Be Child 37

Defense 41

Gift 42

What We Do For Fun Around Here #3 44

No Tamer, No Butcher, No Hunter 45

When A Crop Duster Sees A Body	46
A Destruction Of Cats Discovers You	46
Walking On Water	51
Beard Cycle	52
What We Do For Fun Around Here #4	53
Olive Saloon	54
After Olive, Above Bakery	55
Grandfather	56
What We Do For Fun Around Here #5	57
Smothering Behind The Silos	58
You May Never Meet My Son	58
Guesswork	63
Root	65
A Few Reasons We Left The Farm	66
Growing Up On Grain	68
Grandmother	69
What We Do For Fun Around Here #6	70
My Younger Brother Explains	71
How To Lose A Younger Brother	71
Slaughter	75
About The Author	79
Acknowledgments	81

PASTURE

Tired at last with prayer, I leave my bedside
and stalk the farm with an old wooden bat

murdering lightning bugs and envisioning angels
in fatal flutters—wings smeared across

the sky. Handfuls of crushed abdomens still dimly lit
I rub on my face and palms like war paint. Anointed,

I swing feral at the moon and stars
picturing a frightened god and his fragile

son in their crumbling dim plunge.
Nebraska night compresses around each blow,

begins the slow burial of bodies, blame. My mother
is pronounced into the clearing suddenly, quietly,

thin layers of nightgown covering her body.
I point to the dark empty sky,

the slaughter in the pasture,
my thin sweaty chest.

APOLOGY

Maybe it was my neglect that allowed the bald-faced
hornets to build their first nest under your eaves
out of pulverized barn and spit. My excuse then:

the flimsy ladder, an allergic reaction, no grasp
of how to maintain proper romantic relations.

When they found their way into your attic
under a window I swore I had closed,
I should have approached with a wooden

bat or can of spray, but instead let it be
until winter, hoping the cold would swallow them up.

I know now that I was mistaken, with these nests,
frigid gray breaths, hanging from every branch of every
tree, these nests howling in the belly

of your walls, under your front porch, in the recurring sting
of words, each of us blindly protecting ourselves.

FISHING

You drag the snapping
turtle a quarter mile
by its tail after snagging
it on your hook in
the irrigation pond.
It weighs over half
your weight, twists
itself clockwise,
counter-clockwise,
tears holes in your jeans,
snaps at the heels
of your shoes, hisses
at your hands and your edible
face. Mom slaps you
when you show her
to avoid fainting. Dad
helps you haul the claw-
foot tub from the neighbors'
trash heap, fill it from the garden
hose, and slide in the snapper.
You lose interest in an hour
and run off to the hayloft to hang
on the rope swing. The beast
arches its neck, bites the air
into smaller air twigs, and glares
up at our parents. *I could digest
his body before the next full
moon. I would devour each of you
soon after.* Before you return, they lift
the snapper from the tub, secure him
to a snow shovel with thick twine,
and drag him back down to the pond.

AT ONE HUNDRED, A MIRACLE

Mother found you sobbing
in our plastic swimming pool
nearly buried in dead toads.

You cradled all you could,
maybe thirty or forty
blistered bodies. The rest
piled against your ankles
and slipped under your feet
when you finally tried to stand.

Once you called them each by name,
tamed them with coos, croaks,
and whispers, wiped your arms
in the gift of their urine, were
welcomed into their family, fed
them, worshipped with them,
and offered them a home.

Dad and I dumped the bodies
into the incinerator and hosed
down the pool shivering
against the garage
door while you gasped
to Mother, *I didn't mean to
let the sun get so
hot, I forgot
to move them to
the shade, I
only wanted to see
what happened
at one hundred.*

I suppose it is true that while preaching
addition I also spoke to you of God.
When you asked, *what happens
at one hundred?* I held the answer
in my mouth like a miracle, water now
wine, made you wait to taste it,
whispered like the second
coming, made you beg for it,
then at last described the shape,
the sound of ninety-nine
finding one hundred.

And you only six,
began one, two, three,
four. You collected sticks
and stones, bottles
of every color and
shape, abandoned
sparrow nests, snake
skins, and rusty nails,
but nothing happened.
When you asked, *why
has nothing happened*, I said
you have to count the living

for the rapture to occur.
With you still spelling brother
b-e-l-i-e-v-e, you began searching
for life. When you found one
hundred you could hardly hold him.

With time though, all boys stop
believing. A week before you found them
dead you left them waiting
for you, counting the days,
the lifetimes until you returned.

NIGHT SHIFT

I sway on a stranger's front porch
holding a beer I no longer want.
It is somehow four a.m. Across the road
construction equipment leans
into the night. A man appears
cradling a six-pack, a shotgun
slung over his shoulder, a scowl
already loaded with scotch.
We finish our beers staring
from either side of the road.
We open another.
When his six-pack of High
Life is finished he aims
his gun—at the trucks
filled with dirt, the stop
sign on the corner, each
stranger's mailbox, the moon, me.
He points his shotgun at me,
holds it for a minute,
ten minutes,
forty-five. A train
siren. An hour. I suppose
I should be afraid. I open
another beer. At ten a.m.
he puts his shotgun away,
kicks his cans under
the nearest truck, nods over to me,
and leaves back the way he came.

THERE'S A BEAST ROAMING

there's a beast roaming
your property,
passed through my land
yesterday. tore the living right out of
my livestock. you have
a gun? need to keep it
loaded, well-greased, and hung
beside your back door.
board over the front door and
windows. that will have to do.
if we had more time
we could have cut down
those thick pines,
opened up our sight
from the porch out to the crops.

hell
you should board up that barn,
keep your chickens
up on the second floor,
the goats too. children?
you have children.
sure as shit he'll eat the children.
goddamn it, i can smell
the son of a bitch
in the air, like a tire
factory explosion,
rubber melting through
flesh, hunting down the bone.
do you have any
baking
powder,
fishing wire,
old rags
or dresses?
no matter, take handfuls of manure,
rub it all over your
body. i'll be back
in a day
or i'll be gone forever.

THE ARCHITECTURE OF OBSESSION

this shirt
was born into my wardrobe
twelve years ago, stolen from the closet of
my first lover's sister. my skin
within the fabric
forever
seeking out the sun.
in the right lighting you can
see my nipples wrapped in
silk and slowly dying.
in the right lighting you can see
that same ex-lover dismantling
her own web for nourishment,
swallowing each thread she crafted
the day before. the most intricate fort
was built around a beekeeper
and her four hives of bees.
i stole her hair for years
while she slept
(one strand at a time)
and fashioned them into four walls
and the roof above her,
a key (which i swallowed)
that trapped her and her bees
humming in me forever.

my fascinations clamber over
the tin roof of my partner's
fort. she imagines herself on a sailboat.
future lovers looming
on the threshold as
collisions waiting to occur.
they imagine themselves as thunder clouds,
as chosen ones, as dust settling, as hands
rising from lakes to wave me closer, but
they are all hornet's nests trembling
branches. or
i am the hornet's nest and
they built me out of silk and spit
and a collection of abandoned forts.

BREAKING

My body was still without shape in third grade
and I ached to carry a ball the way he did, tossing
sixth-graders off his haunches like loose earth, galloping
for touchdown after touchdown and neighing loudly.

We shot hoops at the abandoned gym
in fifth grade, returning home
with dust matted in our manes, stuck
to our skin, our spit dark-brown.

His fingers were ferocious, always snapping
at me, so I never took a shot or spoke,
instead spent the night feeding him
the ball, tallying my assists. Each basket
the rim swallowed like a sugar cube.

Shot after shot, finally he named me
friend, and all evening I shivered
when we brushed bodies, when he pressed
me on his way to the rim, when he placed
the bridle gently in my mouth.

Tenth grade, I thought I broke
free from him, shooting
across the middle of the field
following a well-thrown spiral.
When my feet lifted from the
ground and the ball grazed my palms

he approached abruptly from behind,
dove through my knees, and spun me
like a hay bale onto my collarbone
which popped, a distant gunshot.

I quit team sports our senior year
choosing instead to run
long-distance. Father grounded
me indefinitely, and called him
to save me from myself,

but when he approached this time
I did not flinch. When he moved
towards me, when we touched, I shook
him off and began to gallop.

MOTHER

Faith still rooted
though trunk split
twice by lightning.

*Six brothers remain and one
sister*, you say. *My children
but one, both parents,*

*and my husband still
alive. And this tree, look at this
tree, even now growing.*

WHAT WE DO FOR FUN AROUND HERE #1

We could hike the mile
over to the junk heap and
toss rocks at the rats.

DEATH/WISH

When you leap from the hay-
loft again, Brother,
please land this time
on your feet.

Death will always be the wrong fort
for an eight-year-old
to hide within.

When you leap from the hay-
loft again, Brother,
please assume

that bottle must have been buried
beneath the hay you fell into
on all fours that afternoon.

When you rose from the hay
wrists out, your skin
opened like a piano
lid, strings and levers

exposed. When your fingers pressed
on keys, we both waited for a sound.

The last time we raced the living
room, your right big toe swallowed
a sewing needle hidden in the shag

carpet. In the backseat, your foot
propped up, brown thread trembled
out of your skin like the tail
of a rat just eaten. When the doctor

explained the needle was bent,
he would need to slice your toe
in two to remove it,
I wondered if the rodent
he was sure to find
would still be breathing.

When you leapt from the hay-
loft, did my hands wait
to basket your fall, my fingers
woven brambles,

or did I attempt to build death
out of my hands, releasing
your hands too soon?

When you tumble from the hay-
loft again, please
forgive me, Brother,

I must have been buried
beneath too many layers of
my own skin to stop myself.

When you rose from the hay,
wrists out, my skin
opened like an emergency
room, doctors and nurses

exposed. When your fingers pressed
on me, I did not dare make a sound.

The day before we raced the living
room the last time, I nearly swallowed
a sewing needle, held it in my mouth

and called it a key, a trembling finger
propped against the back of my throat,
let it penetrate my skin, brown thread
curling on my tongue. When Mother

entered the room, I spit the needle
out quickly into the brambles
of carpet, explained with eyes
bent what needed to be said
to remove her from the room,
but still could not catch my breath.

SUMMER

This year-old beard, the beers
in my fridge, the sadness hibernating
in my body like a family of bears
will not survive the summer months.
I will chew off layers of my face
with dull scissors, and send the hair
in green glass bottles to my closest
friends. With these same friends
I will share the beer sweating
through evenings singing in the
sunroom. And the bears will leave
the cave to rollick and rampage,
to seek out food for the winter
cold, and will only return home
when their stomachs are filled
and snowstorms hunt the sky.

ON YOUR BIRTHDAY

We will wait for you in the sun
room. A blue-jean quilt hangs
over my head and droops down
to the floor. I sip cheap port
and wear Apple Juice
as an eleven-pound cod
piece with claws. She whispers up
sweet nothings and insists I speak
the same phrases to you when you return.
It starts to snow. I hold a damp warm
dish towel to my puffy left
eye and hope the stye will
disappear before you dump me.

I picture your blurred nude
body fluttering between
the bedroom and the hallway
closet, preparing for work
this morning.
Did you slip hips
into a swarm of hornets
or black under-
wear? Did you
try on a total solar eclipse
or just a warm winter
coat? When did you start
dangling butterfly cocoons
from your ears? Did you notice me
squinting between the sheets,
pretending to sleep?

I should have kissed you open-
mouthed before you left,
instead of twisting my neck
and offering you my ear.
I should have leapt from the bed
and lashed my limbs to your calves
in impossible sailor knots
then forced you to learn how
best to untie me before you left.
I should, at least, spend the rest
of the day scratching at the door
properly waiting for your return.

WHAT WE DO FOR FUN AROUND HERE #2

Drag used lawn mowers
behind Dad's truck until they
dissolve into dirt.

FATHER

I sit alone in my apartment, sipping cold
miso soup from a coffee mug. And you

will sit alone in your apartment after drifting
through small Nebraska towns, once again

failing to make a sale. You will debate retrieving the remote
that rests cold across the room on a stump of end table.

MY FATHER EXPLAINS HIS BIRTH

I don't remember much, only
what I've been told by your granddad.
it was 1949 maybe,
on a farm outside some no-name town,
at least an hour forty-five drive
from Omaha, days after
a tornado flattened
half the state, picked up
whole cities and
set them down.
I must have been
fifteen or twenty
pounds newborn,
full of holler, a dark
head of hair,
but when they found me
I was half-starved,
naked, and white as a winter
field, curled up in a flipped pig feeder,
looked like a grounded rocket
ship leaning against
your granddad's fence post.
he didn't own any hogs,
hell, he didn't even own
the farm, drove a bus
for a living, but took it
as a sign, brought me in,
named me Charles
after my granddad, and asked
around, but we never found
my real parents. they
must have been swallowed into
the belly of
that twister.

TO MY FIRST LOVE'S SOON-TO-BE CHILD

your mother, speaking of baby seagulls,
said at times they leap from cliffs careless,
or maybe they were born
to test their wings that way,
and they have no choice but to jump.
I wonder if you will be born
folded up with my face, my name,
words offered to your mother, and
will be unable to
unfold them
from your flesh.
the last time I wept
I did not think only of her, all
vessel now, a
a ship you boarded silently,
hid within
for months
in the cargo
between two potato sacks, not yet a boy,
unsure of where you were traveling, just a
movement when she couldn't sleep beside
your father.
the last time I wept it was over
a ghost of you,
a hallucination of you,
you standing perfect
next to your mother, asking her, who
is Benjamin Charles?
should we keep those journals of his?
those boxes of letters
are taking up space.
should I toss them into
the dumpster?
and she responds, yes.

DEFENSE

With both left and right eyelids now infected,
and my only glasses broken, I blink
across state lines at you. You
sit quietly, or pace compelled, or
frown and smooth your sheets to perfection,
or pull the quilt over your head and call
it tent, cave, Atlantis, belly of a whale.
You lift the phone to call a friend, maybe
me, before noticing how long your feet
appear, poking from your sheets like fence
posts. You rumble your toes and call it earthquake.
You kick like wild and call it tornado.
The phone dangles in your hand for days,
hangs from your fingers forgotten, some humming
ghost, before you pull the cord from the wall, let out
a roar, and hurl it from your bedroom window
into the yard below. This is how I see you
anyway. I apologize
if it is not as clearly as it once was,
but in my defense, my eyes are swollen shut,
and there are years upon years between us.

GIFT

*I wake swallowing feathers. A wandering
albatross shivers agitated in my twin bed,
wings tucked tight against its sides. Molted feathers
lift from the sheets and resist the downward pull
of air. Why am I still here? the bird
finally asks. Will you hang my beak
above your mantle? Will you pluck my wings
and roll in the feathers with friends at dinner
parties, spilling wine, giggling
hysterically? Will you strap
my carcass over your shoulders
and stumble off a cliff, calling it flight?
The Albatross spreads its wings
their full twelve feet, attempts to fly,
but cannot snap the rope lashed to its leg.*

I decide on the drive to school
what to teach to my students.

I leave work at three and slip through
traffic hoping to make it home
in time for a nap.

On the couch I eat Swedish shortbread. Maybe
a high school basketball game is on the screen

but I can't be certain
with the volume only a click or two
above mute and my glasses

across the room. My cat Apple Juice lies motionless
on my lap and farts every four to seven minutes.

I bathe in silence, my bulges rising from the bathwater
like pale, rounded beaches, toes popping
in and out of waves like sea turtles.

My pubic hair drifts like seaweed
and I consider trimming it.

I glance again at the closet
mirror and poke into
my fleshy frame.

I wait for sleep. Untrimmed cat claws
scrape in pursuit across the wood floor

outside my room. Apple Juice kills
a cockroach, paws it back and forth
on the floor, in the air,

then carries it gently onto the bed
and places it on my chest.

WHAT WE DO FOR FUN AROUND HERE #3

Crowd the kitchen, call
it *real talk*, ask all your friends
to speak up at once.

NO TAMER, NO BUTCHER, NO HUNTER

Friends, the poems so far have all emerged
frightened from some forest, furred

or feathered, and impossible
to wrestle down to the wood

floor without force. Embarrassing.
I am without suitable tools to finish

this task. Without a net even, and words
of worth leap from my window

and crawl into the cradle
of the nearest ditch weed.

Are you compelled to capture your poems
this way, or do they flutter

against your face, begging to be
placed into an old jam jar?

WHEN A CROP DUSTER SEES A BODY

accidents will happen when
flying too close to the ground, under
power lines, spraying crops from
fifteen feet or less, dodging grain silos and
the tree line. now
I've been doing this for years
without any hiccups. built my own plane
from the ground up, crop dusting
all the land between the airport and town,
stitching sky to sky to farm properties
miles away, and on call for
wildfires in the prairie
since '79. like I said,
I've been doing this for years, but when
I see the body
nude, shaking against that fence post,
slowly swallowed up by shadows,
I can't tell what
from what, up from
down. the telephone pole suddenly
swiping at my right wing
comes at me like the dead
risen, a starving bear
leaving winter. I have to roll the plane into
an emergency landing
one field over—
I would have died
without years of practice, and
a blessing from God.

A DESTRUCTION OF CATS DISCOVERS YOU

approaching your own body like the dark
corners of the abandoned barn, such fragile
swallowed gestures. only daring
any sound when a train enters
the silence, and then you clear your throat.
shaking off yesterday's stories, told
to frighten you motionless,
by curving your spine against a wooden post,
writhing relived down strings of barbed wire,
a shuddering claim of ownership. your sister's
voice, distant
aluminum echoes, playing tag
in the empty grain bin.
I approach
your body
with a destruction
of others, circling around,
eating up the space,
your smell, each breath now
an unbearably unknown terrain
redefining the boundaries of the sky.
you open your eyes as though you have just
found the click in the lock of
what was thought to be
your darkest room, discovering instead
light, a room full of light.
to witness this act again,
this offering,
a gift to some savior.

WALKING ON WATER

Brother, you say, *run all the way to town
with me.* It is usually too hushed for me
after church services end, after pickups
finish cruising the square, circling like
cicadas mating, after the last flimsy
barn is freckled with a tipsy farmer's
buckshot. *But listen,*

*thunderstorms are hunting the water
towers and stalking the tallest trees
and solitary tractors and I want to run. Mother
will repeat, lightning kills children, until she falls
asleep, and then we can strip
down to our shoes and short
shorts lifted from the locker room
and slip out the kitchen window.*

Conversation would only be crushed
under the plummet of these raindrops,
so I stay silent. *Look at the shuddering
irrigation ponds and the cornfields
choking and sputtering, drowning
all around us.* You name me again
as brother when I finally teach you
how best to assemble your steps

into a sprint, a gallop, or a lope. When
we reach the school track and find it
a sea, you shout, *remember
these bleachers around us, gasping
beached whales pleading for the raindrops
to fall.* When I tire you pull on my arm
until I continue, and I continue though even now
there seems to be no bottom, no end.

BEARD CYCLE

This morning sagging branches,
ripened apples ready to be
plucked, stolen from the

neighbor's orchard. This
afternoon washed in dead
sea mud, pumpkin, sweet

potato, carrot, and
honey. This evening
stuffed plump with

words to prepare
for winter. Tonight
rooted to her

until she blossoms,
until her mouth releases
baskets of its ripe fruit.

WHAT WE DO FOR FUN AROUND HERE #4

Meet at the Olive
kill a keg of Sunshine and
wake up on your roof.

OLIVE SALOON

Brian snaps
his fingers now
to every song,
orders us to
dance for Virginia,
dance for the Rocket
Man, for the Piano
Man. He belts out
each song a beat
too slow, but is

sure of every word
and this dance
floor sermon.
He may as well be
a prophet in this place,
because we are ready
to follow him into morning.
Virginia smiles at Brian as he
plugs the jukebox with endless *play
now*, compliments her sweater vest's
floral print, and orders another

round. The closer we are to last call,
the more often his laughter lands
on us like whooping cranes, squawking
prayers, migrating blessings
choosing to perch here
for the night. Every time he laughs
a friend appears, or another pitcher,
and Virginia smiles when
Brian smiles, and keeps the doors open
until two when she finally sends us
home, humming to herself a hymn.

AFTER OLIVE, ABOVE BAKERY

Lacking enough to flurry
tonight. Your expected call must have
collided with a truck on the way

to my home. I shiver on this
porch, sipping from a bottle.
Gestures once folded

between us, silent offerings of
wine and fingers finding
fingers. Below us

then, within stacked brick,
firewood slumbered
where bread would soon be.

GRANDFATHER

Tonight you may die,
fingers too arthritic to
even grasp your guitar,

trembling and useless,
severed branches of a tree
rattling in a truck bed.

Less than a mile
from the hospital, I drink
wine from a bottle

and do not think of you.

WHAT WE DO FOR FUN AROUND HERE #5

Tall boys, alleyway
wiffle ball, crushed cans line base
path and lead us home.

SMOTHERING BEHIND THE SILOS

        if you burn that bale of hay
to ground, he has reason to ghost you,
            so don't blame me if
           he follows you home.
everything has its place, its purpose.
hauntings aren't any different. they are
put together just like you or me, except
          a ghost bale's grief
won't hold still shivering all night
            behind the silos.
        I'm not a betting man, but

  more must be crossing the fence
     at the edge of the soybean field.
  how many did you already burn?
you call it an accident. still, be careful
you don't cross a field on your own
anytime soon. they will surround you,
a smothering. keep your mouth shut.

they put the devil in your granddad,
           forced an evil spirit in
between dreams. he wasn't the same.
    he left home and only returned
       every three or four months.
         usually it was just to steal
           from the family coop.

YOU MAY NEVER MEET MY SON

tonight, I fear my son's whispers—mouth
small as a kidney bean, fingers unformed,
months away from birth,
a murmuring stone.
I am unable to sleep—skin
smoldering ecstatic or fractured with cold,
afraid even to move from the quilt. I am
days away from a solitary month at sea,
sailing the boat Willow south
to the Great Barrier Reef.
you can have all I own if I die.

can I send M a letter? Your journals
are spirits. now I'm kept awake by the space
between us, though we've not met, though
we may never meet. I imagine
discovering her voice in the flight of
migrating birds, in the slow breath of
her bees always returning to the hive.

I haven't forgiven myself
for breaking our promise. he was all waves
when he came back
to claim me. I won't describe the men
I have lived with since. I can tell you that
it is no longer hard to exit. now, I leave
without telling anyone.

GUESSWORK

When all is right,
I can fly the ocean
like a well-crafted kite

steering only with a twist
of wrists and my fingertips,
string strung from the sea
bed to the spool.

Lately though my limbs
are clumsy and flying
the ocean turns

out to be dangling
a shoelace in the bathtub
and begging the water to rise.

You step lightly a different
shore unaware of this sad sea—
pant legs rolled to the knees,

a bag full of smooth stones
looped to your belt with a hand-
fashioned leather strap. In a basket

made of wicker, your child sleeps
beside you on the shore. Your laughter,
a plunging of Northern Gannet,

somehow does not wake
him, even diving for fish,
emerging from the ocean

so close. You wade
the shallows, skip
pebbles, and persuade

ripples to appear for me
or maybe for no one at all,
but forgive me now

if I repeat your name until I am
convinced you see the ocean
lift up and become the sky.

ROOT

Shape your poem into a warm nest
of dry brushwood and crushed willow
leaves. Let an animal be born
there. Let the same animal
die there. Replace the animal
with family. Replace
death with departure.

A FEW REASONS WE LEFT THE FARM

The mulberry tree we found planted
horizontal in my second-story
window. Roots strangling the twin-
bed I had left for the safety
of the basement hours before.

The old farm wife who did not stop at the stop
sign, instead buried her husband's
truck into the crumble of my father's
Oldsmobile, then blamed shotgun holes
in the stop sign and the height of the corn.

The height of the corn
when we had nothing
to do with growing it.

Grandma pruning Grandpa's
branches and moving into town.
Leaving him to tend her own
apple, lemon, and peach trees,
a garden of rhubarb and spices.

Sugar's spilling
face, dangling red
and white fur clinging to
her jaw. Dog whimpers. Coyotes
attacking in packs.

Siblings sniffling
in packs. Allergies
prowling our bodies
like wild dogs.

The story I told at breakfast
to scare my siblings. The rat
that clambered across the safety
of my quilt the night before.

The same rat that Mom caught
before breakfast in a trap
too small, its top half
still squirming, squealing, until
her iron skillet found its skull.

Dad shaking, sobbing after
burning the leaves and trash
in the incinerator and discovering
our cat's first litter inside.

GROWING UP ON GRAIN

As superheroes we leapt onto buildings
of barley and wheat stacked in your father's
warehouse. Fighting crime kicking jagged
holes into hundreds of fifty-pound bags,
which he found pooling on the cement floors.

You and I, no longer
heroes, blamed the rats.

The next summer we stripped nude and stretched
every roll of plastic wrap we could find
back and forth four feet from the floor,
tucked the edges between bags of corn
and soybeans, and imagined an ocean.

Under our thin plastic wake,
underwater without our
underwear, we swam together.

Just before high school I wanted so badly
to hurt you every time you looked away.
I imagined you stumbling from our shelter,
blood spilling from your nose and between
your fingers like grain.

I left at last without saying a word
or locking the warehouse door,
and tried to swim the gravel
roads back to town.

GRANDMOTHER

Sometimes you prune fruit
trees in the yard, your frail back
bent double with the
burden of three full-grown sons
rooted to your spine, rotting.

WHAT WE DO FOR FUN AROUND HERE #6

In Ditch-Em the goal
is for the front car to lose
the car that follows.

MY YOUNGER BROTHER EXPLAINS

from the long dirt roads
your face still sprouts into
a smile describing those deer
leaping out of
the night following your run
all the way to the airport.
returning to this place,

what will I unearth?
I still draw triangles
as two deer flanking you,
endless movement away from me
(or maybe this is all
lie.
a story I still tell
myself). how finding you was always
impossible. my only clues
the outline of the air
with your body removed,
the mystery mossed over
by shadow that you were
beneath
or behind,
the stalagmites of your

breath discarded. I remember
you staking elder claim to
frogs, fish, and fowl
when only I took the time for naming.
I know how many bats flew
over the year before we left, how many
stayed through the summer,
how many wounded
you left behind the barn.
I know how to tend an animal,
and when to set it free.
I know beetles are what clean the dead
birds of their flesh. I still know
after coyotes, how many stitches

lace a dog's face back together.
You will always haunt clusters of
these steel cylinders, your absence
hovering, the pressure found in
a memory without body.

HOW TO LOSE A YOUNGER BROTHER

there is always something stalking and
something being stalked.
a place for this hunt to occur.
rules scribbled into the earth
with a finger or sharpened stick.
this summer I will be the hunted.
my brother will learn how to hunt,

tripping through the underbrush,
bloodying shins
on barbed wire
and my booby traps.
to escape a younger brother, first
listen for the sudden breaking
of branches, heavy breathing,
a quiver of melody
when he tries to hum away
his fears. stay a field apart
at all times, even when he calls to
you, even when he whimpers
again and again,
brother,
brother,
brother.

your scent,
shake off by sewing through
the pond with swimming,
or climbing high enough
up a tree. now dash
in endless circles
spooking him with owl sounds and
badger growls.
I bet you think he knows me better.
at least to shake my body out of branches
when night approaches. at least
enough to return home beside
me. at least enough
to be surprised

with an offering of mine,
a new unearthing.
I don't know why I'm still out here,
it is exhausting.
my brother is lost.

SLAUGHTER

I only agree to butcher my first sheep
after another argument with my mother.

Dark early, day is dragged
toward its inevitable

demise and I follow my father closely,
silently down the path to the barn,

directly away from my mother's
sobbing, dulled with each step

from her, from the house,
from her house.

Surrounded by pens of sheep looking on
my father teaches me the difference

between a stylet and a spear
point paring knife,

how to crush muscle and bone
most effectively with a cleaver,

the three main cuts of the lamb.
He teaches me the humanity of killing

quickly, with the quivering beast
on his side, my slight knees pressed

against body—blade angled across
his throat, near the jaw, severing the wind-

pipe and bones of the neck, traveling
completely through to the spine.

My hands, his hooves
stop trembling.

The body is skinned, hung
to bleed. My father says quietly,

Look at the quality of his flesh.
How tender it must be.

This proves the character of his pasturage,
the importance of where he was reared.

I follow my father out of the barn,
my outstretched fingers grazing

the thick coarse wool, the wet open
mouths of the rest of the herd.

ABOUT THE AUTHOR

Ben Clark grew up in rural Nebraska and now lives in Chicago, Illinois. He has worked as an English teacher, librarian, tile maker, track coach, and in a microwaveable popcorn factory. Presently he is an MFA student at the School of the Art Institute of Chicago. He also regularly attends the Vox Ferus writing workshops and acts as an assistant editor for *Muzzle Magazine*. This is his first full-length collection of poetry. You can find out more at benclarkpoetry.com.

ACKNOWLEDGMENTS

Thanks to Debra and Apple Juice for all of the love, support, and laughter.

Thanks to Derrick Brown and the rest of the Write Bloody authors for accepting me into the family with such grace and guidance.

Thanks to Debra and Lea for their wonderful design work, Josh for his incredible illustrations, and Todd for his magical cover photo.

Thanks to these journals for publishing some of this work in earlier forms: Muzzle, Bestiary, Stymie, Word Riot, DecomP, and Anderbo.

Thanks to the Vox Ferus Workshop for teaching me how to write, and the Real Talk Live venue and performers for teaching me how to speak.

Thanks to my friends/readers/classmates who made this book what it is. Sherry, Elise, Mary, Ruth, Michael, Janet, Calvin, Rebecca, Erin K., Erin O., Patty, Tona, Jill, Storm, Kate, Marty, John, Laura, J.W., Sarah, Stevie, Emily, Roger, Robbie, Molly, Stacy, James, J.P., Aaron and Emily, Kim, and Kurt.

Thanks to everyone in these organizations for their continued support: The School of the Art Institute of Chicago, Hastings College, the Encyclopedia Show, Mental Graffiti, the Green Mill, Lowitz and Company, Fleet Feet Chicago, the Grind, and the Olive Saloon.

Thanks to these places for being the best places on earth: Chicago, Illinois. Hastings, Lincoln, and Aurora, Nebraska.

Thanks to my family for supporting me no matter the color of my hair, the length of my beard, or the quality of my poetry. Mom, Dad, Andy, Emily, Amanda, Molly, Patrick, George, Jennifer, Ava and Olivia, Grandma, Grandpa, thank you. I love you all.

Thanks to Todd and Cody, Brian, Jordan, Martha, Patrick, Tom, Whitney, Jen, Michael S., Ron, Ted, Amoz, Shannon and Jeremy, Gwynne and William, Joel and Michelle, Joko and Lee, Rachel D., Jeff and Faith, Madison, Michael D., Dan, Matt W., Tyler, Jeremiah, Marnie, Meghan, Michael M, Christina, Jim, Rachel C., Gabby, Pinky, Audrey, Lindsey and Neil,

Virginia, Mike B., Colin, John R., Matt M., Bob, Alexis, Jeff L., Greg, Nika, Amy D., Rik, Kevin, Nate, Marc, Lauren, Cathie E. and Richard S., Linda, Linda and Dennis, and on and on.

Thanks to those friends that I forgot to add to this list. I am sorry. Thanks to anyone who has taken the time to comment on my work. Thanks to those of you who have introduced yourself to me, those of you who have made me laugh, and those of you who continue to stun me with your talent, your honesty, and your compassion. Thank you, thank you, thank you.

NEW WRITE BLOODY BOOKS FOR 2011

DEAR FUTURE BOYFRIEND
A Write Bloody reissue of Cristin O'Keefe Aptowicz's first book of poetry

HOT TEEN SLUT
A Write Bloody reissue of Cristin O'Keefe Aptowicz's second book of poetry about her time writing for porn

WORKING CLASS REPRESENT
A Write Bloody reissue of Cristin O'Keefe Aptowicz's third book of poetry

OH, TERRIBLE YOUTH
A Write Bloody reissue of Cristin O'Keefe Aptowicz's fourth book of poetry about her terrible youth

38 BAR BLUES
A collection of poems by C.R. Avery

WORKIN' MIME TO FIVE
Humor by Derrick Brown

REASONS TO LEAVE THE SLAUGHTER
New poems by Ben Clark

YESTERDAY WON'T GOODBYE
New poems by Brian Ellis

WRITE ABOUT AN EMPTY BIRDCAGE
New poems by Elaina M. Ellis

THESE ARE THE BREAKS
New prose by Idris Goodwin

BRING DOWN THE CHANDELIERS
New poems by Tara Hardy

THE FEATHER ROOM
New poems by Anis Mojgani

LOVE IN A TIME OF ROBOT APOCALYPSE
New poems by David Perez

THE NEW CLEAN
New poems by Jon Sands

THE UNDISPUTED GREATEST WRITER OF ALL TIME
New poems by Beau Sia

SUNSET AT THE TEMPLE OF OLIVES
New poems by Paul Suntup

GENTLEMAN PRACTICE
New work by Buddy Wakefield

HOW TO SEDUCE A WHITE BOY IN TEN EASY STEPS
New poems by Laura Yes Yes

OTHER WRITE BLOODY BOOKS (2003 - 2010)

STEVE ABEE, GREAT BALLS OF FLOWERS (2009)
New poems by Steve Abee

EVERYTHING IS EVERYTHING (2010)
New poems by Cristin O'Keefe Aptowicz

CATACOMB CONFETTI (2010)
New poems by Josh Boyd

BORN IN THE YEAR OF THE BUTTERFLY KNIFE (2004)
Poetry collection (1994-2004) by Derrick Brown

I LOVE YOU IS BACK (2006)
Poetry compilation (2004-2006) by Derrick Brown

SCANDALABRA (2009)
New poetry compilation by Derrick Brown

DON'T SMELL THE FLOSS (2009)
New Short Fiction Pieces By Matty Byloos

THE BONES BELOW (2010)
New poems by Sierra DeMulder

THE CONSTANT VELOCITY OF TRAINS (2008)
New poems by Lea C. Deschenes

HEAVY LEAD BIRDSONG (2008)
New poems by Ryler Dustin

UNCONTROLLED EXPERIMENTS IN FREEDOM (2008)
New poems by Brian Ellis

CEREMONY FOR THE CHOKING GHOST (2010)
New poems by Karen Finneyfrock

POLE DANCING TO GOSPEL HYMNS (2008)
Poems by Andrea Gibson

CITY OF INSOMNIA (2008)
New poems by Victor D. Infante

THE LAST TIME AS WE ARE (2009)
New poems by Taylor Mali

IN SEARCH OF MIDNIGHT: THE MIKE MCGEE HANDBOOK OF AWESOME (2009)
New poems by Mike McGee

OVER THE ANVIL WE STRETCH (2008)
New poems by Anis Mojgani

ANIMAL BALLISTICS (2009)
New poems by Sarah Morgan

NO MORE POEMS ABOUT THE MOON (2008)
NON-Moon poems by Michael Roberts

MILES OF HALLELUJAH (2010)
New poems by Rob "Ratpack Slim" Sturma

SPIKING THE SUCKER PUNCH (2009)
New poems by Robbie Q. Telfer

RACING HUMMINGBIRDS (2010)
New poems by Jeanann Verlee

LIVE FOR A LIVING (2007)
New poems by Buddy Wakefield

WRITE BLOODY ANTHOLOGIES

THE ELEPHANT ENGINE HIGH DIVE REVIVAL (2009)
Poetry by Buddy Wakefield, Derrick Brown,
Anis Mojgani, Shira Erlichman and many more!

THE GOOD THINGS ABOUT AMERICA (2009)
An illustrated, un-cynical look at our American Landscape. Various authors.
Edited by Kevin Staniec and Derrick Brown

JUNKYARD GHOST REVIVAL (2008)
Poetry by Andrea Gibson, Buddy Wakefield, Anis Mojgani,
Derrick Brown, Robbie Q, Sonya Renee and Cristin O'Keefe Aptowicz

THE LAST AMERICAN VALENTINE: ILLUSTRATED POEMS TO SEDUCE AND DESTROY (2008)
24 authors, 12 illustrators team up for a collection of non-sappy love poetry.
Edited by Derrick Brown

LEARN THEN BURN (2010)
Anthology of poems for the classroom. Edited by Tim Stafford and Derrick Brown.

LEARN THEN BURN TEACHER'S MANUAL (2010)
Companion volume to the *Learn Then Burn* anthology. Includes lesson plans and worksheets for educators. Edited by Tim Stafford and Molly Meacham.

WWW.WRITEBLOODY.COM

PULL YOUR BOOKS UP BY THEIR BOOTSTRAPS

Write Bloody Publishing distributes and promotes great books of fiction, poetry and art every year. We are an independent press dedicated to quality literature and book design, with an office in Long Beach, CA.

Our employees are authors and artists so we call ourselves a family. Our design team comes from all over America: modern painters, photographers and rock album designers create book covers we're proud to be judged by.

We publish and promote 8-12 tour-savvy authors per year. We are grass-roots, D.I.Y., bootstrap believers. Pull up a good book and join the family. Support independent authors, artists and presses.

Visit us online:
WRITEBLOODY.COM

www.ingramcontent.com/pod-product-compliance
Lightning Source LLC
Chambersburg PA
CBHW060503080526
44584CB00015B/1528